North American Indians Today

North American Indians Today

Apache

Cherokee

Cheyenne

Comanche

Creek

Crow

Huron

Iroquois

Navajo

Ojibwa

Osage

Potawatomi

Pueblo

Seminole

Sioux

North American
Indians Today

Pueblo

by
Kenneth McIntosh

Mason Crest Publishers

Philadelphia

We wish to thank all the wonderful people who helped us with this book: Will Herrera, Rebecca Bautiste, Julia Herrera, Ruth Koyona, John Ray, Veronica Sarracino, Candice Sarracino, Rose Seyouma, Noreen Simplicio, Cheree Shebala, Ardale Mahooty, Carlton Jamon, Brian Vallo, Dale Sanchez, Vincent Sanchez, and Cubero Elementary Inter-Tribal Dancers. Special thanks to these people, without whom this book could not have been written: Ann Rose Ray, Lena P. Tsethlikia, and the Pueblo of Laguna Tribal Council.

Mason Crest Publishers Inc.
370 Reed Road
Broomall, Pennsylvania 19008
(866) MCP-BOOK (toll free)

First printing
1 2 3 4 5 6 7 8 9 10
Library of Congress Cataloging-in-Publication Data on file at the Library of Congress.
ISBN: 1-59084-676-1
1-59084-663-X (series)

Design by Lori Holland.
Composition by Bytheway Publishing Services, Binghamton, New York.
Cover design by Benjamin Stewart.
Printed and bound in the Hashemite Kingdom of Jordan.
Photography by Benjamin Stewart. Photos on pp. 21, 62, 64, 74, 79 courtesy of Northwestern University Library.

Contents

===

Why is it so important that Indians be brought into the "mainstream" of American life?
I would not know how to interpret this phrase to my people.
The closest I would be able to come would be "a big wide river".
Am I then to tell my people that they are to be thrown into the big, wide river of the United States?

Earl Old Person
Blackfeet Tribal Chairman

Introduction

In the midst of twenty-first–century North America, how do the very first North Americans hold on to their unique cultural identity? At the same time, how do they adjust to the real demands of the modern world? Earl Old Person's quote on the opposite page expresses the difficulty of achieving this balance. Even the common values of the rest of North America—like fitting into the "mainstream"—may seem strange or undesireable to North American Indians. How can these groups of people thrive and prosper in the twenty-first century without losing their traditions, the ways of thinking and living that have been handed down to them by their ancestors? How can they keep from drowning in North America's "big, wide river"?

Thoughts from the Series Consultant

Each of the books in this series was written with the help of Native scholars and tribal leaders from the particular tribe. Based on oral histories as well as written documents, these books describe the current strategies of each Native nation to develop its economy while maintaining strong ties with its culture. As a result, you may find that these books read far differently from other books about Native Americans.

Over the past centuries, Native groups have faced increasing pressure to conform to the wishes of the governments that took their lands. Often brutally inhumane methods were implemented to change Native social systems. These books describe the ways that Native groups refused to be passive recipients of change, even in the face of these past atrocities. Heroic individuals worked to fit external changes into local conditions. This struggle continues today.

The legacy of the past still haunts the psyche of both Native and non-Native people of North America; hopefully, these books will help correct some misunderstandings. And even with the difficulties encountered by past and current Native leaders, Native nations continue to thrive. As this series illustrates, Native populations continue to increase—and they have clearly persevered against incredible odds. North American culture's big, wide river may be deep and cold—but Native Americans are good swimmers!

—*Martha McCollough*

Breaking Stereotypes

One way that some North Americans may "drown" Native culture is by using stereotypes to think about North American Indians. When we use stereotypes to think about a group of people, we assume things about them because of their race or cultural group. Instead of taking time to understand individual differences and situations, we lump together everyone in a certain group. In reality, though, every person is different. More than two million Native people live in North America, and they are as *diverse* as any other group. Each one is unique.

Even if we try hard to avoid stereotypes, however, it isn't always easy to know what words to use. Should we call the people who are native to North America Native Americans—or American Indians—or just Indians?

The word "Indian" probably comes from a mistake—when Christopher Columbus arrived in the New World, he thought he had reached India, so he called the people he found there Indians. Some people feel it doesn't make much sense to call Native Americans "Indians." (Suppose Columbus had thought he landed in China instead of India; would we today call Native people "Chinese"?) Other scholars disagree; for example, Russell Means, Native politician and activist, claims that the word "Indian" comes from Columbus saying the native people were *en Dios*—"in God," or naturally spiritual.

Many Canadians use the term "First Nations" to refer to the Native peoples who live there, and people in the United States usually speak of Native Americans. Most Native people we talked to while we were writing these books prefer the simple term "Indian"—or they would rather use the names of their tribes. (We have used the term "North American Indians" for our series to distinguish this group of people from the inhabitants of India.)

Even the definition of what makes a person "Indian" varies. The U.S. government recognizes certain groups as tribal nations (almost 500 in all). Each nation then decides how it will enroll people as members of that tribe. Tribes may require a particular amount of Indian blood, tribal membership of the father or the mother, or other *criteria*. Some enrolled tribal members who are legally "Indian" may not look Native at all; many have blond hair and blue eyes and others have clearly African features. At the same time, there are thousands of Native people whose tribes have not yet been officially recognized by the government.

We have done our best to write books that are as free from stereotypes as possible. But you as the reader also play a part. After reading one of these books, we hope you won't think: "The Cheyenne are all like this" or "Iroquois are all like that." Each person in this world is unique, whatever their culture. Stereotypes shut people's minds—but these books are intended to open your mind. North American Indians today have much wisdom and beauty to offer.

Some people consider American Indians to be a historical topic only, but Indians today are living, contributing members of North American society. The contributions of the various Indian cultures enrich our world—and North America would be a very different place without the Native people who live there. May they never be lost in North America's "big, wide river"!

The Pueblos' ancient heritage is a part of their identity today.

Chapter 1

Beginnings

Keshi!
("Welcome" in Zuni)

In many ways, Zuni, New Mexico, is like other American cities. People carry cell phones, surf the Internet on their home computers, and drive new-model trucks or imported sedans. Kids wearing jeans and T-shirts walk to school lugging their books in backpacks. Basketball is a favorite sport. You can stop at the Route 53 Café and order soda, burgers, and fries.

At the same time, Zuni is unique. For starters, the Zuni people speak their own language—a language used by no other people on earth. Unlike other cities, most of the people of Zuni are artists or craftspeople. Some Zuni live in centuries' old homes with **adobe** mud walls. Fresh bread is baked in outdoor earthen ovens. Many Zuni follow spiritual beliefs practiced by their ancestors thousands of years before Europeans came to the Americas. The Zuni are one tribe of today's Pueblo Indians.

When Europeans arrived in what is now the American Southwest, they found people living in adobe villages. Multistoried apartments, ceremonial courtyards, and water sources were carefully arranged in each town.

Route 53 Café in Zuni serves both common foods and unique Zuni specialties.

Impressed by these *pueblos* (Spanish for "towns"), the Europeans called the Southwestern Native peoples "Pueblo Indians."

Today, there are nineteen different Pueblos in New Mexico. Another Pueblo group, the Hopi, live in Arizona, and the Tigua live in Texas. Though they share similarities, each group has its own unique language, spirituality, and culture. This book relates the lives and experiences of many different Pueblo Indians. Do not assume that what is true for one group or person is true for another. The first inhabitants of the Southwest are people of great diversity.

Their spoken traditions tell Pueblo Indians who they are and from where they came. The importance of these oral traditions is seen at the A:Shiwi A:wan Museum and Heritage Center in Zuni. There, a tribal member stands in front of a beautiful mural and explains the Zuni's traditional story of their *emergence* into the world. She describes the Zuni's journeys to the place where the people still live today.

At first, the world was empty: no people lived on its surface because the *A:shiwi* (People) lived in an underground world of darkness. Then the Sun Father sent the *Ahayu:da* (Twin War Gods) to the underneath world to lead the people upward. The people climbed up through the starlight world, the moonlight world, and the dawn world. They emerged into this daylight world at Ribbon Falls, in the Grand Canyon.

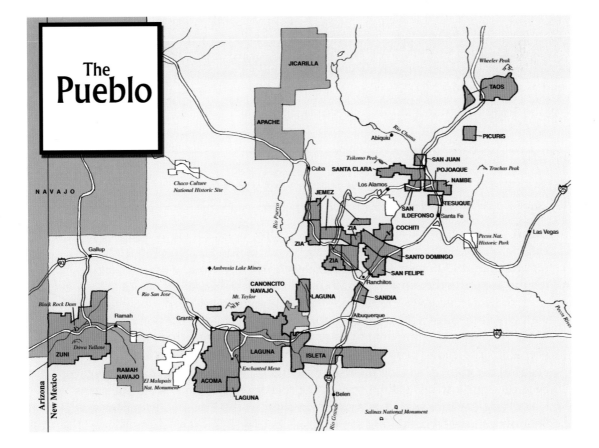

Place of Refuge

Dowa Yalanne (Corn Mountain) is an enormous, beautiful mesa adjacent to Halona (Zuni), south of Route I-53. The broad flat top towers a thousand feet (approximately 305 meters) above the desert floor. According to tradition, priests led the people to the top of Corn Mountain during the Great Flood. As the waters rose, they discovered to their horror they had nothing but corn. They had nothing with which to make necessary sacrifices. Seeing their peril, the son and daughter of the chief priest volunteered to be the sacrifice. Prayer feathers and food were prepared. The young people dressed in their best outfits and stepped off the steep edges of the cliff, sacrificing themselves so their people could live. Their bodies became stone and can still be seen in the rock formation known as "the twins." Dowa Yalanne later served as a safe retreat when the Zuni had to escape from Spanish military forces during the 1680s.

When the people first saw themselves in daylight, they didn't like what they saw. After living so long underground, they looked like animals. The Ahayu:da changed them to the way people look today and taught them how to make offerings and live in harmony with the earth.

After the people had adjusted to life above ground, they began their journeys to Halona (the Middle Place). At Daturah Mound, the War Gods offered a choice of two gifts: a dull-colored egg and a turquoise blue egg. At first, people ran after the prettier egg. Those who weren't so fast got the dull egg.

After the people had chosen one gift or the other, the eggs hatched. The dull egg produced a brilliantly colored parrot, which led its group to the Lands of Everlasting Sunshine, now Mexico and Central America. The colorful egg produced a crow, which led its people to the East.

The group following the crow traveled until they came to a great river flowing from north to south. The War Gods warned the people, "These are magical waters. We don't know what will happen when you cross, so whatever happens, cling tightly to the children who are crossing on your backs."

The people started across the water, but in the middle the parents felt

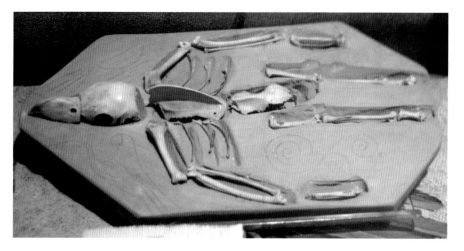

Archaeologists found the remains of a Central American Macaw at Hawikku, showing that the people who settled in Zuni remained in contact with their relatives who journeyed to the "Lands of Everlasting Sunshine" in the south.

Pueblo Indian ceremonial chambers are called kivas. A kiva is entered through a hole in the roof, a reminder of the hole through which people entered this world from worlds beneath.

Kachinas are spirit messengers, represented here by wooden figurines.

something cold on their backs. Looking over their shoulders, they saw that their children had taken the shape of turtles, frogs, and fish. The parents were afraid and let go of their children, and the children became the amphibians that inhabit the world today.

Warned by the experiences of the first group, the second group to cross held onto their children despite frightening changes in their appearance. When they reached the other shore, their children were normal again.

The first group hated to leave their children behind in the river, but that night they heard strange sounds. The War Gods investigated; when they came back, they reported to the grieving parents that their children were dancing and singing with joy. This river became the place of the Kachinas, the spirits that still visit the Pueblo.

The people traveled on to Hard Scrabble Wash, where the Coyote Society was playing drums. The people danced to their drumming. After the dance, they separated the people into groups, like families. The people

Our Land

"This has always been our land. We know these matters not merely because our grandparents told us vague stories when we were children, but because our parents and grandparents, and their parents and grandparents before them, made sure to tell us so exactly and so often that we could not forget."

—Elders from Zia, Jemez and Santa Ana, in a 1950s' land claim

Kokopelli is frequently pictured in the rock art of the Ancient Ancestors. He is now a popular figure used by many Southwest artists. Kokopelli was a humpbacked flute player known for his trading, tricks, and sexual affairs.

were asked to name an animal or a plant they would like to represent their group. This is how the clans originated, and to this day the people are all members of clans.

When they reached the Village of the Great Kivas, the people were tired of traveling. They asked the War Gods to help them find the Middle Place. They called on the water strider to stretch its legs all the way to the four oceans. The water strider said, "Wherever my heart lands, that is the Middle Place." Its heart landed at Halona, the Middle Place, today known as Zuni.

This story comes from the Zuni; the oral histories of other groups are different, but they all have some things in common. For instance, Pueblo people share a sense of permanent connection to the land. They also feel connected to their ancestors and the past.

A century ago, people spoke of the Pueblo as "vanishing American

Ancient ruins remind today's Pueblo of their rich past.

When Edward Curtis took a picture of this Hopi girl a century ago, he assumed Pueblo Indian culture would soon vanish. Despite many attempts by non-Indians to destroy their lives and culture, the Hopi and members of twenty other Pueblos are flourishing today.

Indians." Today, they are far from vanishing! They have successfully fought to regain lands, sacred *artifacts*, and respect from non-Indian neighbors. As long as the *mesas* and canyons of the Southwest endure, the Pueblo people seem likely to remain and prosper in their ancestral homes.

The Ancient Ancestors of today's Pueblo Indians are sometimes called the Anasazi. The Anasazi left scores of impressive ruins, like this one at Bandelier National Monument. Some of today's pueblos began as long ago as these ruins, but they were never abandoned and continue to be lived in today by people who have kept their language, culture, and spiritual beliefs alive for many centuries.

Chapter 2

The Ancient Ancestors

Irritated by the insects swarming around its thick red fur, the mammoth waded into a pool and filled its trunk with water. As the gigantic beast began to spray itself, its enormous ears caught an unfamiliar sound. Instantly, a dozen figures sprang up from the reeds surrounding the pond. Straining their muscles, the half-naked men swung their atlatls, or throwing sticks. Their spears swooshed through the air, and razor sharp *obsidian* tips sliced through fur and tendons toward the huge elephant's vitals. The mammoth roared, shuddered, and then sank down into the bank. The hunters yelled and clasped one another in joy. None had been injured, and their clan would eat well for many days to come.

We can only imagine such scenes, for there are few remains left behind by the most ancient people of the Southwest. The first people in New Mexico and Arizona were wandering hunters. Scientists call them "Clovis"

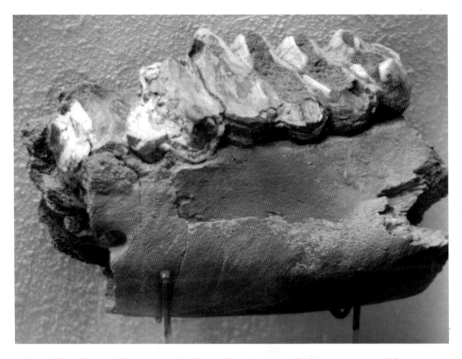

The molar of a woolly mammoth, found at Zuni, is all that remains of these gigantic elephant-like beasts who once lived throughout the Americas and were hunted by the ancestors of today's American Indians.

people, because their large stone spear points were first found at Clovis, New Mexico. They hunted wooly mammoth, giant bison, and other large game. Scientists have suggested that these people came across a land bridge connecting Siberia and Alaska some twelve thousand years ago, but recent discoveries have cast doubt on that theory. Instead, the Pueblo's ancestors may have come by boat from Asia, or possibly Europe. Most Pueblo people deny having origins outside of North America.

After thousands of years living as hunters, people learned how to grow corn in the dry desert land. Since they now needed to stay in one place to tend their fields, the Southwestern farmers began to form permanent communities. These people, called the Mogollon, lived in semi-underground homes with doors on top of the roof. Their pit houses were similar to the kivas used for ceremonies by modern-day Pueblo Indians.

More than two thousand years ago, the Southwestern farmers developed a highly sophisticated culture. They built grand adobe cities in the

An ancient dwelling at Bandelier National Monument.

Pottery found at Hawikku demonstrates the artistic skills of the ancestors of today's Zuni people.

sides of cliffs and atop mesas. Some of these pueblos, such as Chaco Canyon and Mesa Verde, are now monumental ruins. Others, such as Taos and Acoma, continue to be lived in today. Scholars refer to these ancient city builders as *Anasazi*, a Navajo word meaning "ancient enemies." Many Pueblo Indians prefer to call them "ancient ancestors."

The Ancient Ancestors were impressive engineers. For example, Pueblo Bonito, in Chaco Canyon, contained more than six hundred fifty rooms and forty kivas; parts of it once stood five stories high. Sky City, in Acoma, contains more than nine hundred separate homes that are still inhabited today.

As impressive as the cities are, so are the roads made by the Ancient Ancestors. Covering over four hundred miles and amazingly straight, they linked what are now three states. Archaeologists are unsure why these roads were built, because the Ancient Ancestors did not use wheeled transportation. Placed at intervals along the roads were watchtowers where fires at night could be used to communicate over vast distances.

The Ancient Ancestors also mastered agricultural techniques. The Hopi Indians today joke that they chose to live in dry mesas because no one else would want to farm there, and they could live in peace. They are among the best dry farmers in the world, and their skills are a tribute to the *ingenuity* of their ancestors.

Before Columbus sailed, more than a hundred communities lived in peace with one another in the American Southwest, growing food and producing highly sophisticated crafts. They maintained a trade network extending all the way down to Central Mexico and west to the Pacific Coast. Their astronomical knowledge rivaled that of any other civilization. At the height of their culture, they never suspected that their world was about to be invaded.

In 1539, Marcos de Niza set out to explore the American Southwest. He returned with fanciful tales of the Pueblo Indians' vast wealth. Some say he saw sun shining like gold on pueblo walls. Others say it was really pottery mixed with *mica*, which appeared to be golden vessels. In any case, the Spaniards' lust for gold brought them to New Mexico in force. In 1540, Francisco Coronado rode into Zuni with his *conquistadors* in their glittering armor. He slaughtered twenty people at Hawwiku.

Lena Tsethlikia enjoys showing visitors to Zuni petroglyphs pecked into rock around A.D. 1100 by Zuni ancestors.

Ancient petroglyphs at the Village of the Great Kivas illustrate the migrations and beliefs of the Anasazi people.

In 1598, Juan de Onate, the first Spanish governor of New Mexico, arrived. He decreed that Spaniards could steal food, shelter, and clothing from the Indians. In response, warriors from Acoma slew several of Onate's men—and Spanish troops armed with cannon, muskets, and swords were sent to punish this revolt.

The Indians had never faced such weapons. They tried to surrender, but the Spanish were determined to make an example of them. The Acoma people were pulled from their houses and thrown over the side of a cliff. Men, women, and children sought refuge in their ceremonial kivas, but the troops set these afire. Many were burned alive. In the end, a thousand Acoma were slaughtered.

The five hundred who remained alive faced further torment. Men had their right foot cut off as a form of punishment. The women served as slaves in Mexico for twenty-five years.

After the conquistadors, came the Spanish missionaries. Some Indians welcomed the Catholics, and churches were built in the pueblos. The San Estaban del Rey church in Acoma, for example, was begun in 1630. It was a massive work built from twenty thousand tons of earth and stone that were carried from the canyon floor up the steep sides of the mesa. Forty-feet long logs for the upper beams were carried by hand over twenty

The first Europeans to meet Pueblo Indians brought death and enslavement as they sought after nonexistent gold treasure.

Although some Pueblo Indians welcomed Christian missionaries, they came to resent the mistreatment they received from the priests and other European settlers. Today, most Pueblo Indians combine Catholicism with their traditional beliefs, but the ancient ways are regarded as the more important of the two.

mountainous miles, and they never touched the ground. Fourteen years later, the church was finished.

A painting of Saint Joseph was brought to the church from Spain, and before long, people reported the Saint had performed miracles of healing. When nearby Laguna was struck by drought, the Acoma lent them the painting and rains returned.

Although some early contacts between the Europeans and the Indians were positive, the harsh practices of Spanish **domination** fueled Indian resentment. The Pueblo people were virtually slaves, forced to work for Spanish landowners. Indians were burned alive for practicing **traditional** beliefs. Spanish soldiers raped Indian women. Men were **lynched** or taken as slaves.

The Past Comes Home

Until the 1960s, scientists assumed they had the right to unearth ancient objects and remove them to faraway museums. Older people in Zuni remember wagonloads of boxes being taken from the village by archaeologists in the 1920s. In fact, more than 20,000 items were removed from an ancient part of Zuni called Hawikku. This village was an ancient pottery-making center, located along a trade route used by the Ancient Ancestors. In 2003, a group of these items were returned to their community. When Zuni met with representatives of the Smithsonian Institution, the museum's representatives agreed to bring seventy of the remarkable pots and other artifacts back home. It rained as the boxes were unloaded in Zuni, but no one was unhappy. The Zuni understand rain as one form in which their ancestors visit the earth, and no one doubted the ancestors were pleased.

The Pueblo Indians had endured eighty years of such treatment, and they could suffer no longer. After a *medicine man* named Popé, from the pueblo of San Juan, was flogged by the Spanish, he held secret meetings and sent messengers to all the pueblos. They united in a plan to revolt and agreed to strike on August 10, 1680. The leaders of each pueblo were given strands of leather with knots to be untied, one each day, to count down the days until the attack. It was an incredible feat, secretly coordinating the efforts of 17,000 people—who spoke different languages and held different customs—all under the watchful eyes of their oppressors.

On the appointed day, six thousand Pueblo warriors attacked their Spanish overlords throughout the Southwest. Soldiers, landowners, and priests were killed. The Spanish retreated to Santa Fe, where they held off the warriors for a week. The Indians then allowed survivors to retreat into Mexico. The Pueblo Indians granted mercy to the Spaniards, even though the Spaniards had never shown such mercy to them. Today's Pueblo Indians sometimes refer to the Pueblo Revolt as "the First American Revolution."

The Spanish returned to New Mexico a decade after the revolt, but they came back with an improved attitude. They no longer claimed the right to help themselves to the Indians' possessions. Trading took place, and churches were rebuilt in the pueblos.

When the Navajos and Apaches attacked, some Pueblo joined forces with their Hispanic neighbors to defend their land. Unfortunately, contact with whites also brought the deadly *smallpox* virus to the Pueblo. The Indians lacked any *immunity* to this disease (which was new to North America), and the sickness claimed many Indian lives.

New Mexico changed ownership in 1846, when the United States took possession from Mexico. Since the United States was busy establishing its rule over the Apaches and Navajos, the new government ignored the Pueblo. One exception occurred in 1847, when a group of Indian and Hispanic people assassinated the state's governor. Only a few Indians were involved, but the government retaliated by slaughtering 150 Taos Indians and burning their church.

An exhibit at Hawikku illustrates a twentieth-century deception. Archaeologists promised the Zuni that human burials would be undisturbed when they dug there, yet over a thousand human remains were removed to museums in the East.

Lena Tsethlikia holds a pot she made. It is modeled on an ancient piece unearthed at Hawikku in the 1920s and recently returned to Zuni. Hawikku was a pottery-making and trading center of the Anasazi. The people of Zuni are proud to carry on the artistic legacy of their Ancient Ancestors.

In the late nineteenth century, the Pueblo faced a new wave of assault. This was not a military invasion: new railroads brought swarms of scholars, tourists, and Indian agents to the Southwest. Cheap novels and spectacular shows had excited America's curiosity about the so-called "noble savages" who lived in the West. Some people came with friendly motives, other came to take advantage of the Indians, but the overall effect was harmful.

In 1879, an *anthropologist* named Frank Cushing moved to Zuni to learn the language and customs. He was welcomed and even adopted into a clan, but he ultimately failed to respect the sacred ways of his hosts. By showing disrespect to their holy objects, Cushing broke an important Zuni *taboo.*

Meanwhile, the Hopi were subjected to Reverend H. R. Voth, a missionary who wanted to learn all he could about Hopi customs in order to show how foolish they were. He barged into private and sacred ceremonies and took pictures without permission. Hopi today still despise him.

By the turn of the century, tourists, museum collectors, and traders were *pillaging* the pueblos for pottery, jewelry, woven blankets, and sacred spiritual objects. At times, this trend was beneficial to the Pueblo, since Indian artists were able to sell their crafts to an eager market. There was also a dark side to the Indian trade market, however, as sacred objects were stolen from places of worship to be sold.

While white people were busy removing objects of art from the Pueblo, the people themselves suffered catastrophic illness. Whooping cough, smallpox, measles, and *diphtheria* swept through the villages in repeated plagues. By 1900, the population of all nineteen pueblos had been reduced to barely more than a thousand people.

At the same time, Pueblo people faced a new attack on their culture: federal government boarding schools. The motto of these schools was, "Kill the Indian in order to save the child." Indian children were taken from their homes and forced to live in dormitories far from home. Their hair was cut, they were made to wear non-Indian clothes, and they were punished for speaking their own languages. *Epidemics* spread through the dormitories, and children died. To this day, many Pueblo Indians recall with sadness their experiences at boarding schools.

November 21, 1934, brought momentous change to the Pueblo. When Congress passed the Indian Reorganization Act, it required Indians to form tribal governments with written *constitutions* and elected officials in order to be eligible for government assistance. This worked well for tribes whose governments were similar to the new model, but poorly for those whose traditional ideas of leadership differed.

During World War II, thousands of young Pueblo men went to serve in the Armed Forces or work for the war effort in the factories. Tribesmen from Taos Pueblo were the first code-talkers. Their Indian dialects provided an unbreakable code that proved critical for defeating the Japanese in the Pacific.

Serviceman Santana Romero survived prison camps and some of the most terrible events of World War II. In later years, he became governor of Taos Pueblo. Though men like Romero served their country well, the veterans who returned home in 1945 were still not able to vote. New Mexico did not allow Indians to vote until 1948.

In the 1950s, the atomic age created demand for nuclear fuel; the largest deposit of *uranium* in the United States happened to be on land bordering Laguna and Acoma pueblos. The Anaconda mining company paid the tribes for mining rights and employed Indian workers. An enormous mining pit dug in Laguna eventually yielded more than 24,000,000 tons of uranium-rich ore. The radiation from the mines caused illnesses, but money from Anaconda also gave the people economic opportunities they would not have had otherwise.

Around the same time, companies sought to mine coal from land owned by the Hopi. In 1966, the Black Mesa mines were given permission by the Hopi government to extract 400 million tons of coal from tribal lands. To this day, the tribe is divided as to whether this is a blessing or a curse. The mines bring money—but many believe that they *desecrate* Mother Earth.

In the 1960s and 1970s, after years of education designed to destroy their languages and beliefs, Indians boldly declared allegiance to their traditions. Local Indian-run schools began to replace boarding schools. Indians fought in courts for their lands and the right to practice their religious beliefs.

The last years of the twentieth century saw a series of victories for Pueblo people. Museums returned stolen sacred objects to the Zuni. The Pueblo also gained water and land rights.

Some Pueblo found a new source of money from gaming. In 1982, for example, the Acoma opened Sky City Casino. Money from the casino has helped them buy back over 400,000 acres (162,000 hectares) of their traditional lands. Pojoaque Pueblo opened Cities of Gold Casinos in 1995. By

A display at Bandelier National Monument shows an Anasazi woman at work in her home. The Ancient Ancestors built apartment complexes with hundreds of living units combined to provide protection and efficient community life.

combining the casino with a hotel, golf resort, and other businesses, this small pueblo has become the second largest private employer in New Mexico.

It may seem like a long journey from the Ancient Ancestors to today's Pueblo Indians, but today's Pueblo and those of the past are more closely connected than you might imagine. Despite five hundred years of warfare, torture, disease, and government education, Pueblo people hold fast to their languages and spiritual beliefs. At every evening meal, they set a small amount of corn in a bowl. This is then burnt, or set in water, as an offering to their ancestors' spirits. The Ancient Ancestors continue to dwell in the hearts of Pueblo Indians today.

Each pueblo possesses a cane given by President Abraham Lincoln as recognition of their status as sovereign nations. Political representatives of the pueblos carry these on special occasions.

Chapter 3

Today's Pueblo Governments

"As long as you keep a good heart, you always win. Because good overcomes evil." Those are the words of Verna Williamson, quoted in Stephen Trimble's book, *The People*. Verna is a woman whose **optimism** has enabled her to face many difficulties and to triumph for the good of her pueblo. In 1986, she became governor of Isleta Pueblo, making her the first woman governor of any pueblo. More recently, she has pressured the Environmental Protection Agency to clean up the Rio Grande River, which runs through her pueblo. She has been described as tough yet compassionate, traditional yet able to work effectively in the modern political world.

Before running for governor, Verna sought advice from her tribal elders. They told her, "The government came to us from the Spanish. This is recent history, only three or four hundred years ago." They saw no conflict, however, between modern government and the ancient and sacred ways. Looking toward the future, Verna says, "I see so many good, intelligent

Good Leaders

"Office holders must not be argumentative or stand out in public debate; they must not drink or be public nuisances; they must not fight; and above all, they must have good hearts."

From *Zuni Religion and Philosophy* by Edmund Ladd.

young people who have so much potential, I can hardly wait for them to be involved in tribal government."

Tribal leaders need to be optimistic, because leadership is no easy job. On the one hand, their purpose is to preserve the beliefs, practices, lands, and resources their people have held for generations. At the same time, they must be politically and technologically *savvy* in order to represent the needs of their people in the twenty-first century. Tribal leaders need to fight against outside interests and at the same time, create *consensus* within their own communities. It is a difficult balancing act.

Before the European invasion of the Southwest, each pueblo had well-organized systems of self-government, as well as efficient legal systems. During the years of Spanish occupation, the Pueblo adapted to the "governor system." Each village selected a governor, who served as a *liaison* between the tribe and the Spanish government. At the same time, clan mothers and spiritual leaders exercised unselfish authority over the everyday lives of their people.

In 1863, President Abraham Lincoln provided each pueblo with a cane. These canes are still revered and held ceremonially today by the Pueblo governors. This gift symbolized "the perpetual acknowledgment and commitment of the United States" to honor the right of self-rule for each pueblo. In short, Lincoln affirmed that the Pueblo could make and enforce laws over their own people and lands.

The Indian Reorganization Act of 1934, the brainchild of John Collier, Franklin D. Roosevelt's Commissioner of Indian Affairs, was a significant change for Pueblo governments. Known as "the Indian New Deal,"

Collier's policy encouraged tribes to adopt written constitutions and elect councils.

Tribal councils today have great power and responsibility in their communities. They protect the land and water rights of the tribes against outside interests. They negotiate with federal, state, and local governments, as well as with businesses and private parties. They make laws for the tribe, oversee land use, and watch over businesses and charitable organizations. In short, they are involved in almost every major matter within tribal borders.

One important responsibility of tribal governments is deciding who are members of the tribe. The U.S. Supreme Court has ruled that each Indian tribe must determine who its members are. In 1978, Julia Martinez brought a lawsuit before the Supreme Court against Santa Clara Pueblo. She was a full-blooded member of the Pueblo who had married a Navajo Indian with whom she had several children. Two years before this marriage, the Pueblo passed a membership law excluding children from membership in the tribe if their father was not a Santa Claran. Although the Martinez

Will Herrera served as tribal secretary for the Pueblo of Laguna in 2002, and treasurer in 2003.

The Offices of the Pueblo of Laguna Tribal Government contain the tribal council chambers and many services essential to the community.

children were raised on the reservation, they could not vote or hold office because they were not tribal members. The Supreme Court upheld the rights of the tribe against the Martinez children, saying: "Membership rules are a mechanism of social self-definition, and as such are basic to the tribe's survival."

Requirements for tribal membership vary from pueblo to pueblo. One factor is an individual's percentage of Indian blood. Some tribes require only one-eighth Indian ancestry, others as much as half. Also important is the percentage of blood from that particular tribe and whether the father or the mother was a tribal member. Issues of membership become important in political campaigns and in deciding who gets money from federal aid or tribal business profits.

In some tribal governments today, members elect councils and officers. At Laguna, the tribal council serves as the governing body of the tribe, similar to a state government. Laguna tribal members elect a twenty-one-member council that includes the governor of the pueblo, first lieutenant governor, second lieutenant governor, treasurer, secretary, and other officers. Two members are elected from each of the six Laguna villages to make up the rest of the tribal council. All councilmen serve a two-year term. Each village also elects *majordomos* to care for village roads and other properties. These officers may also settle local disputes.

Frequent village meetings offer the pueblo opportunities to discuss issues being presented in the council. Members of Laguna Pueblo tend to be more involved than most Americans are in the political decisions affecting their lives.

Other pueblos are less broadly *democratic* than Laguna. At Acoma, for example, men do the work of government yet serve at the pleasure of the clan mothers. The women of the Antelope Clan appoint tribal officers: the governor, lieutenant governor, secretary, treasurer, and so on. If they wish, the men appointed may leave office after their term has expired. They may also be removed if the clan mothers perceive them to be failing in their duties.

The Hopi have struggled to balance traditional and modern elements of government. In keeping with the requirements of the Reorganization Act,

The Importance of Elders

"OUR ELDERS, preserving OUR PAST in their memories, influencing OUR PRESENT when we dare to listen, aiming us toward OUR FUTURE, rooted in their wisdom, they deserve our respect. Elders are valuable resources to the Pueblo and custodians of tribal history, culture and tradition and they are the best hope of the Pueblo to pass on the Pueblo's history, culture and tradition to children of the Pueblo."

From the Pueblo of Laguna Tribal Government Profile.

Rebecca Bautiste gives a warm welcome to all the people who come through the entrance of the Pueblo of Laguna Tribal Government Building.

the Hopi Tribal Council was formed in 1936. The council was supposed to represent all Hopi in dealings with the U.S. government.

The Hopi constitution, which came with the council, introduced the idea of majority rule. Consensus was the Hopi tradition—all persons agreeing, rather than the larger party winning over the smaller. The new way of majority vote was upsetting to many of the people.

Today, the tribal council deals with matters outside the tribe, but the twelve separate Hopi villages remain semi-independent from the council. Only three villages have adopted constitutions. Oraibi remains strictly traditional in government and will not accept funds or any form of assistance from the tribal council. Other villages combine modern and traditional styles of leadership. They appoint a traditional village leader yet also send representatives to the tribal council.

Traditional Hopi see each village as a complete and independent government. The village leader is called *Kikmongwi* and is head of all religious

and nonreligious authority. Although the Kikmongwi sounds pretty power-
ful, his power is actually limited because traditional Hopi decision-making
is based on community consensus rather than any one person's authority.

Clans also play an important role in village leadership. A council of clan
leaders advises each Kikmongwi. These leaders interpret religious teach-
ings that concern villagers' personal behavior.

While each pueblo governs itself, there is also the All Indian Pueblo
Council. Before the Europeans came, the various pueblos had cooperated
to improve trade and defend against common threats, and today's pueblos
work toward the same spirit of cooperation. In 1922, the nineteen New
Mexico pueblos began meeting to discuss the effects of government poli-
cies. In 1965, the All Indian Pueblo Council drew up a formal constitution.
Since then, they have been working together for the common interests of
all the pueblos.

This ancient kiva at Bandelier National Monument is similar to those used in all the pueblos today. Kivas are used for teaching children traditional spiritual beliefs and for sacred ceremonies. Since the Pueblo have suffered much from non-Indians trying to steal or destroy their cultures, what happens inside the kiva is never shared with outsiders.

Chapter 4

Spiritual Life Today

How would you feel if someone entered the church or synagogue where you worship and stole the most sacred objects in the church? How would you like it if a group of strangers barged in on one of the most private and holy moments of your life, talking loudly and taking flash photographs? What would you think if your important beliefs were made fun of all the time in movies and TV shows?

For centuries, outsiders have been stealing, interrupting, or making fun of Pueblo Indian spiritual beliefs. This is especially painful since spirituality is very important to many Native Americans. They do not practice a religion restricted to one day of worship or one place of worship; instead, Indian spirituality encompasses all of life, every day.

Today, Pueblo Indians may not appear "traditional" to their non-Indian neighbors. They dress, drive, and work in ways similar to the culture around them. But in their hearts, traditional ways are there throughout the day. The Pueblo may make corn offerings to the ancestors at each day's start and at suppertime; the Pueblo reflect on how their actions affect the

earth, the Creator, and the spirits of their people; and the Pueblo try to keep a "good heart" in every situation.

Men learn traditional spiritual ways in the kivas. These are underground or semi-underground rooms with an entrance on the top and a ladder descending inside. Usually these structures are round, though in Acoma, kivas are square to save room in the crowded mesa-top village. In Zuni, after the Spanish built a church atop a kiva, the people decided to make their kivas rectangular; that way, a kiva would blend in with houses and the invaders would not be able to distinguish a kiva from a regular house.

What goes on in the kivas is never spoken of outside. In the kivas, young men learn from their elders the prayers, songs, ceremonies, and traditions of their people. Women are rarely (or never in some pueblos) allowed in the kivas. Instead, women learn traditional beliefs from older women. (See the importance of clans in the next chapter.)

Traditional dances occur at set times each year and are celebrated in the *plaza*. The songs, prayers, and dances of each pueblo are unique to that tribe. Dances are a physical form of prayer, interactions with the invisible world. These dances focus on the essential elements of life in a dry land—the need for rain, for healthy crops, for blessing throughout the seasons.

Some traditional dances involve Kachina dancers, who represent the spirits of the ancestors. Dancers during the ceremonies give dolls shaped like Kachina to children. As youngsters learn the meaning of the various Kachina, they also learn how to care for the earth. According to the Hopi tribal Web site, the Kachina "are spirit messengers who send prayers for rain, bountiful harvests and a prosperous, healthy life for humankind. They are our friends and visitors who bring gifts and food, as well as

---

Joyous Life

"The Zuni believes that everyone carries within himself his own personal "life road." Personal conduct in this life assures a smooth and long road—that is, a long and healthy life. It is often said by the elders of the tribe, "There is but one joyous life—you should love each other."

—Edmund Ladd, *Zuni Religion and Philosophy*

The Cubero Elementary Inter-Tribal Dancers under the direction of Mr. Vincent Chavez present traditional dances of Acoma and Laguna pueblos. Mr. Chavez says each dance is a prayer, and every step and motion has meaning. He insists that students who participate in the group must have good grades and good behavior.

messages to teach appropriate behavior and the consequences of unacceptable behavior." There are over two hundred and fifty different types of Kachinas representing various beings, from animals to clouds.

Carved Kachina figures are popular items at Indian craft stores throughout the Southwest. Such carvings were not originally intended for commercial purposes, however. Originally, the figures were carved out of cottonwood root and were symbolic prayers for rain, since the cottonwood tree searches out water.

Shalako is a Zuni ceremony that takes place during the first week of December. Shalakos are giant messengers of the Rainmakers, and Shalako dancers in their attire are an impressive ten feet tall. Spiritual leaders set the exact date for the ceremony forty-five days ahead of the event, but participants practice all year to perform their duties. Each year, seven families who have built new houses volunteer to welcome the "Shalakos." Great amounts of food are prepared for both residents and visitors. Before the great event, feasts are held to honor the men who will be Shalako dancers. The ceremonies themselves are spiritual and athletic feats. Shalako brings the old year to a close and welcomes the New Year, asking for special blessing on participants.

Traditional Native religion is not the only spiritual practice among the Pueblo. For five hundred years, traditional Pueblo ways and Roman Catholicism have existed side by side in the Southwest. Many Pueblo people feel allegiance to both ways, though traditional beliefs hold the upper hand. As one *matriarch* of the Acoma put it: "Acomas are 98 percent Catholic—and 100 percent traditional." A person from Zuni explained: "I do go to mass at the church on Sundays—unless there is a traditional event going on; then everyone goes to that." Bernadett Gallegos, a San Juan and Hopi Indian, says: "As we hold dual citizenship as United States citizens and as members of our

Pictographs near Zuni pueblo portray Kachinas sacred to that Pueblo.

This pictograph near Zuni, New Mexico, portrays a Shalako.

particular villages, we also hold dear our two faiths—that of our ancestors and that of the faith brought to us over four hundred years ago."

Churches are prominent landmarks at many of the pueblos. For instance, San Estaban Mission, in Acoma, dominates the ancient village of Sky City. The church ceiling is a towering seventy feet high, and the walls are ten feet thick. In the old days, it did double duty as a fortress during Navajo or Apache raids. In front of the church is the cemetery, where the ancestors have been gathered together for more than four hundred years. No pews or other seats are inside the San Estaban Mission Church, only a carefully swept dirt floor. This allows room for the sacred dances, which are held there annually. The Acoma feel a special closeness to San Estaban (Saint Stephen) who was stoned to death for his faith; they too have suffered for

When the people of Laguna emerged into this world, they were told they would know their final destination, Kawaike, or Natural Lake, by the sign of a cross. The people witnessed this sign in the year 1699 when a Franciscan Friar, carrying a cross, arrived with intentions of uniting with the people. Mission San Jose de Laguna was dedicated to Saint Joseph and built in that year. The people of Laguna have worshiped there since that time. The altar of the church is decorated with very old and beautiful Laguna art.

A member of the Cubero Elementary Inter-Tribal Dancers is dressed in the attire of an Eagle Dancer. The eagle is the bird that flies highest, so he is closest to the Creator. That's why eagle feathers are used for prayers. There are Eagle Clans at Acoma and Laguna.

their particular beliefs. Saint Joseph is also revered at Acoma, as his painting has been the vehicle of miraculous healing and much-needed rains.

The Pueblo also **venerate** Kateri Tekakwitha, even though she is not yet an official saint. Kateri was of the Mohawk Indian nation in upstate New York. In the seventeenth century, she became the first of her people to embrace the Catholic faith. The Pope recently beatified Kateri, which means the Catholic Church is almost ready to declare her a saint. She would be the first North American Indian to be given this honor. In Pueblo churches, statues of Kateri stand near the altar, often with corn meal in bowls honoring her.

Most pueblos hold yearly feast days honoring Catholic saints, such as San Lorenzo Feast Day, celebrated August 10th; St. Augustine Feast Day on August 28th; St. Anthony's Feast Day in June; and St. Paul's Feast Day in January.

Our Lady of Guadalupe Church in Zuni Pueblo testifies to the two faiths of the Pueblo people. The church was founded in 1629 but had fallen into disrepair by the 1960s. In 1966, when the pueblo and officials of the Catholic Church agreed to restore the church together, Alex Seowtewa was asked to paint figures of Zuni supernatural beings on the inside walls of the church. For decades, he and his sons have been painting life-sized murals of Kachinas inside the sanctuary. The murals have been photographed for magazine articles and television shows, bringing world fame to Seowtewa and Our Lady of Guadalupe Church.

Today, Pueblo Indians talk little about their spirituality. Some ceremonies are off limits to nonmembers of the Pueblo. If traditional ceremonies are open to the public, they cannot be photographed or videotaped. Guests are reminded not to clap or talk during sacred events. These restrictions are ways the Pueblo have learned to preserve what is most important to them.

Non-Indians have threatened Pueblo sacred ways for centuries. White scholars, like Cushing and Voth, pried into the customs of the Indians in order to write books and earn fame. Doing so, they failed to show respect for the beliefs they wrote about. Tourists crowded the pueblos on feast days. Due to the rudeness of non-Indian tourists, pueblo residents were unable to see or hear during some sacred ceremonies. Many sacred items have been stolen; for example, the Zuni War Gods, who are caretakers of the health and harmony of the entire community, were stolen from their mountain shrines for sale to art collectors. (See chapter one for the importance of the War Gods.) At Acoma, an entire chandelier was stolen from inside San Estaban Church. The Hopi suffered theft of their sacred Kachina masks. Tourists have even dug in village cemeteries to steal things.

Despite the old expression that imitation is the sincerest form of flattery, imitation may in fact be neither sincere nor flattering. Pueblo Indians have seen non-Indians and non-Pueblo Indians aping their ceremonies and beliefs in harmful ways. Until the 1960s, novels, movies, and TV shows portrayed Native American ceremonies as "savage rituals" and demeaned the people's dances and beliefs. More recently, Indian spirituality has become very popular with non-Indians. Moviemakers may include Native spirituality in their films in order to be cool, yet they rarely understand what they portray. *New Agers* dabble in Native ways. People write books and even charge money for seminars, claiming to be Pueblo spiritual leaders when in fact they are nothing but frauds; some are not from the pueblos, and some are not even Indian. And still, tourists are rude and annoying as they flock to the pueblos, seeking to take part of Native spirituality home with them. The Pueblo people are warm and gracious hosts, and they do have much to share with the rest of the world—but please be respectful of their privacy and ways when you visit their communities.

Candice and Veronica Sarracino, along with little Roland, live in Mesita, a village that is part of Laguna Pueblo.

Chapter 5

Social Structures Today

Do you ever feel lonely and wish you had more people around to whom you could relate? Have you ever wished you had one place you could always return to and call home? Would you like to have your whole community come out and cheer for you when your school team plays? If you were a Pueblo, you would have all those things. The Pueblo Indians today are strongly connected to family, clan, and community. This enables people of all ages to experience a sense of belonging, support, and community strength, which many non-Indians have never experienced.

Veronica and Candice Sarracino are sisters, young women who live in the village of Mesita, which is part of Laguna Pueblo. When asked who their hero is, both answer: "our mother." She is a role model and a source of strength for the entire family.

Like most Pueblo Indians, the Sarracino family has three generations in the house. If families are not in the same building, they usually live nearby, but it is not unusual to have grandparents, parents, children, and grand-

children living together under one roof. Aunts and uncles may also share dwellings. The Laguna word for "aunt" is the same as the word for "mother," because aunts play an important role in raising their nieces and nephews. Traditionally, aunts and uncles were the ones to discipline children, rather than the parents, which was said to make it easier for children to relate to their own parents.

Pueblo homes immediately tell visitors that these people care deeply about family connections. Rows of family pictures are on the wall of almost every Pueblo household—baby pictures, family portraits, pictures of the kids' sports teams and awards, pictures of graduations, weddings, and family members in the Armed Services. There are often mounted animal heads as well, always accompanied by a story about how the father, uncle, or grandfather brought this trophy home. Art objects, such as pottery, drums, beadwork, or rattles, also hang in the living rooms; family members made many of these, often for special occasions. Ribbons, trophies, or awards, usually for sports or art show prizes, are prominently on display.

In addition to their ties to blood family, Pueblo Indians have deep roots in their clans. Clans, or groups of families, are the basic social units of

Pueblo Indian homes usually have hunting trophies taken by a family member and many pictures of family on the walls.

Candice Sarracino received a special high school graduation gift—a fabulous pot made by her Aunt Susan.

Pueblo Indian life. The origins of the clans go back in time before the Ancient Ancestors built their great pueblo cities. Clans are named after animals or natural forces: eagle, antelope, deer, corn, sun, sky, and so on. When Pueblo Indians are getting acquainted, they often ask: "What clan are you?" People tend to be impressed by membership in clans that have traditional leadership roles in the tribe.

The top row of Candice's pot portrays clan symbols: the sun and corn.

Although men have traditionally held political office, women's place in the clans reflects their importance in Pueblo society. Pueblo are matriarchal; this means that women hold power in the social system. Clan membership is traced through the mother's side of the family. A person is "big clan" on the mother's side and "little clan" on the father's side.

At Acoma, the youngest daughter in a family owns all the family property, since the youngest daughter will live the longest and gain the most wisdom. So, when the family property needs repair, or is going to be rented, the brothers have to ask the youngest sister for her approval before anything is done. Government at Acoma is also matriarchal. Women of the Antelope Clan, assisted if necessary by the Eagle Clan, appoint tribal officers. If they disapprove of their actions, the women can also remove council members.

Within a clan, all members are "brother" or "sister" to one another. For this reason, people cannot marry within their own clan. When Pueblo Indian young people meet and like each other, the first thing they want to know is: "What clan are you?" In small pueblos, it can be difficult to find a mate who is not related to a person's big or little clan. For this reason, people often choose marriage partners from other pueblos. Marrying non-Indians is discouraged, because marriage outside of the clan system means the children will not belong to a clan.

> "Nobody on his own strength has ever succeeded. You need the spiritual assistance, the guidance of those who have gone before."
>
> —Zuni saying

Pueblos tend to do things together. Weddings, funerals, baptisms, and graduations are community affairs. Sports are big, especially baseball; a lighted baseball diamond gets priority in community development. Athletes are known and admired by other members of the tribe. Pueblo Indians are especially noted for being long-distance runners.

When a Pueblo sports team goes to championship level, the entire village comes out to cheer for them. When the team returns, banners greet them. If a member of the tribe has an opportunity to travel abroad for a sports or dance competition, they are funded by grocery store raffle sales. If someone is ill or hospitalized and needs funds, the community chips in for that as well.

With this sort of community closeness, crime is not much of a problem. If someone in the tribe does something, others know about it and will talk to him or her.

Although the term "Pueblo Indians" originally referred to clustered villages such as Old Taos Pueblo or Sky City, many members of Pueblo tribes do not live in their ancestral villages. In some tribes, half the tribal members live off Pueblo lands. Some go to bigger cities in the Southwest, such as Albuquerque or Gallup, to find work. Los Angeles and San Francisco are also home to many Native Americans. Those living in the cities are known as "urban Indians."

Despite the fact that many live away from the pueblos, people come back home to participate in village ceremonies, feast days, or important events involving family or community. A sense of being truly at home, of connection, of always being welcomed and accepted, brings urban Indians home to the Pueblo time and again throughout their lives. Many are also "in and out" Indians, living for a while in their ancestral villages, for a while in the city, or commuting back and forth on a regular basis.

Sky City, Acoma, has not changed greatly in 80 years since this picture was taken. Most Acoma live in modern housing in nearby villages, but a few still live year round at Sky City. It is America's seventh most popular tourist attraction and is overrun with visitors during the day. After the crowds leave at night, residents enjoy a peaceful, traditional life in their ancient hometown.

Even though few Southwest Indians today live in their ancestral adobe homes, Sky City, Old Taos Pueblo, and some of the ancestral Hopi villages are still inhabited. These lack electric power lines, running water, and modern septic systems. Crowds of tourists, who are led through the pueblos in tour groups, overrun Sky City and Old Taos Pueblo during daytime hours. Some residents put up tables to sell crafts or have small shops in their homes. Otherwise, they keep curtains drawn over their windows to retain some small element of privacy. In the evening, when the tourists are gone, they can enjoy a simple, quiet, healthy life in places where their ancestors have lived for almost a thousand years.

Most Pueblo Indians, even those living within tribal lands, live in modern homes. Typically, these are ranch homes, finished with **stucco**, resembling the traditional adobe style. Rooms are built with open spaces connecting dining and living areas. Some homes are heated with wood stoves, others with gas furnaces. Kitchens must be well equipped, so the homeowners can cook for many guests during feast days.

Many Pueblo Indian men hunt the elk, deer, antelope, mountain lion, bear, turkeys, and small game that live on tribal lands. Hunting is not just a sport but also a means of feeding the family and neighbors. To manage wildlife carefully, tribes will issue permits by lottery if game is scarce. When a hunter has killed a deer, the family greets the animal and expresses gratitude. The whole neighborhood is then invited to come share the meal. Women gather together and cook the meat. Then the aunt of the hunter is given the choicest part.

Many homes still have traditional *hornos*, or beehive-shaped ovens, built outside, next to the house, for baking bread. The form of these ovens is very ancient; similar hornos were used at Mesa Verde a thousand years ago. Baking traditional bread is hard work. The dough must be mixed late at night. It is kneaded at three the next morning. After sunrise, the fire is started. By noon, the wood has turned to coal, and the oven should be properly heated. There is no thermometer, so the breadmaker must have a fine sense of the correct temperature. The loaves of dough are set into the oven with long wooden ladles. Finally, by early afternoon, the finished bread can be removed from the oven. In most villages, a few women bake

It is very time consuming, but many Pueblo Indians today still cook bread in traditional earthen ovens, called hornos.

Clothing styles have changed since Edward Curtis took this picture of a Hopi woman making pikki in 1922. However, Curtis' description of how pikki is made is just the same way it is made today.

Rose Seeyouma makes pikki bread at Zuni Pueblo. She is a cheerful person who obviously enjoys what she does. She listens to recordings of ceremonial singing in the Zuni language while she works. Not everyone can make pikki—it is very easy to burn it or splatter the thin paste.

for the entire community. Traditional breadmaking is a lot of work, but it tastes much better than bread bought at the store.

Another age-old custom is baking pikki. Pikki are thin sheets of blue corn flour, folded in a square and served for feast days and Shalako meals. They are used like tortillas, to eat stew. As with many traditional activities, cooking pikki must be done in a prayerful manner. Before beginning, the baker must pay proper respects to her ancestors. The blue cornmeal is baked on top of a large flat stone, set atop a wood oven. Boiled cow brains and shortening smeared on the stone keep the cornmeal from sticking. The pikki maker uses her bare hands to spread cornmeal on the heated stone. If her hands move too slowly, or if she pushes too hard, she will be burned. If

Julia Herrera, of Laguna, is a retired school principal, but she has no trouble finding valuable things to do.

she is not careful, the dough will splatter. When finished, the pikki is paper-thin. It must be removed from the stone very carefully or it will break. Baking pikki is a food-making art.

Not long ago, a spectacular meteor shower brightened the New Mexico skies. A thousand feet (approximately 305 meters) above the desert floor, the residents of Sky City were spectators from atop their mesa. They lay on blankets on the roofs of their adobe homes, watching the heavenly show faraway from electric lights or pollution. Living where their ancestors have lived for more than a thousand years, they enjoy a clear view of the stars, as well as spectacular sunrises and sunsets.

Dale Sanchez, a matriarch of the Acoma, knows and enjoys the simple life of Sky City—but she has also traveled abroad. She and her husband

have a home in Albuquerque, where he works, as well as ancestral property atop Sky City. She enjoys living the traditional way, even though Sky
City lacks what many people would consider necessary conveniences. The
lifestyle there enables people to show their respect for the Earth Mother
and for one another. She says: "I'm glad to have lived in both times—the
traditional and the modern. They both have much to give."

Noreen Simplicio makes Zuni pottery like her ancestors but adds a contemporary twist. On top of her traditional pots she adds a band of clay with highly detailed Pueblo homes and people. These miniature figures are realistically painted and detailed. Her work combines the best of old and new ceramic skills.

Chapter 6

Artistic Achievements

Ruth Koyona's hands pinch and rotate a glob of gray-black clay. Her fingers work quickly, precisely, yet with strength, and the clay seems almost magically to acquire the form of a half-circular bowl. She reaches into a tightly packed desk, pulling out a gourd scraper fitted perfectly for the next task: shaping this piece.

Ruth works in her living room, near the front door. Her home is both a place of family togetherness and an art studio. As she continues to form the clay vessel, her face conveys a sense of contented awareness. For Ruth, this process of creating traditional Laguna pottery is not only art; it is an act of spiritual devotion.

Like many Pueblo Indians, Ruth learned her craft from her parents. She remembers her mother making pots and selling them to tourists along old Route 66. Today, like the work of many Indian artists, Ruth's pots are both a source of pleasure and a supplemental income.

An amazing number of Native people throughout the Southwest are artists. Some are construction workers, or teachers, or engineers—but when the subject of art enters a discussion, they reveal that they also make jewelry, or sculpt *fetishes*, or do beadwork. This is one way the Pueblo people have dealt with centuries of uncertain economic opportunity. Their parents told them, "Jobs may come and go—we can't always control those opportunities—but if you continue the family crafts tradition, you will always have something to fall back on."

Pueblo Indians have attracted international fame and attention for their artistic achievements. This is ironic, considering some of them have no word for "art" in their language. The craft items created by Pueblo Indians today are amazingly similar to the objects of beauty made by their Ancient Ancestors a thousand years ago. The Ancient Ancestors did not, however, see themselves as "artists." They made objects for practical purposes and made them in harmony with the earth and their human community. *Practicality*, *harmony*, and beauty were inseparable parts of making something the right way.

Some of today's Pueblo Indian artists work in contemporary *mediums*. Lee Marmon, for example, who lives and works in Laguna, is famous for his photographs of Pueblo subjects. Zuni artist Alex Seowtewa and his sons have worked for three decades painting murals inside Nuestra Señora de Guadalupe Church, at Zuni. These elaborate paintings portray nearby landmarks, the four seasons, and life-size Zuni Kachinas. The church has been called "the Sistine Chapel of the Americas." Dan Namingah, a Hopi, is another prestigious artist, known for his abstract acrylic paintings.

Other artists take traditional mediums and give them contemporary twists. Roxanne Swentzell, of Santa Clara Pueblo, sculpts clay figures. Her piece titled *Vulnerable* is a nude male blindfolded with an American flag. Diego Romero mixes his Cochiti Pueblo heritage with an urban upbringing in Berkeley, California, and education in Los Angeles. He makes pottery that mixes ancient Greek and ancient Pueblo Ancestor images, then places them both in twenty-first–century settings. A Romero bowl, for example, titled *Bush vs. Bin Laden*, portrays President Bush as a cowboy with a six-shooter. Bin Laden is on the opposite side of the bowl, in a camouflage jacket holding an AK-47. Cartoon bubbles separate the two, with words "Blam," "Bang!" and "Ouch" on them.

Most Pueblo artists, however, continue to work in traditional ways. Al Qoyawayma, for instance, is a highly respected engineer who can be found talking with executive managers in corporate America—and he is also an acclaimed Hopi potter. One of his pots, *Into the 21st Century*, portrays an astronaut holding a golf club greeting Kachina dancers.

Ruth Koyona makes traditional Laguna pottery.

Clay bowls, jars, and canteens express elements of life that are important to traditional Pueblo Indians. These vessels hold water, which is the most valued life-giving substance for people who have lived for centuries in the desert. Seed pots and jars contain corn, the staple of agricultural life. Clay itself is seen as a gift from Earth to her children.

Around A.D. 700, the Ancient Ancestors began making spectacular painted pottery. A group known today as the Mimbres painted on their pots beautiful and sometimes humorous pictures of people, animals, birds, fish, and insects. The Indians living at Mesa Verde in ancient times made black and white pottery with finely painted lines breaking into geometric patterns. The Hohokam made unpainted pottery, which was fired to a lustrous red finish. Pueblo Indians continue to make pottery with the same shapes, finishes, and designs used by these Ancient Ancestors.

Until the last century, Pueblo pottery was unappreciated by non-Indian society. In 1915, though, San Ildefonso potter Maria Martinez was a big hit at the San Diego World's Fair. She and her husband Julian created a beautiful, shiny black style of pottery similar to that of their Ancient Ancestors. Artists and collectors clamored for Maria's pottery. Around the same time, Hopi potter Nampeyo was gaining worldwide attention for her traditionally painted pots. The fame of these two potters led to a worldwide market for Pueblo Indian pottery.

The first step in traditional pottery making is gathering the clay. Each potter has his or her favorite site, where earth provides just the right raw materials. Prayers and corn offerings are made before the clay is respectfully removed.

The clay must then soak in water, so the hard pieces will soften to an even consistency. Then temper is added. (Temper is a substance added to clay to strengthen it.) Ruth Koyona gathers broken pieces of pottery left centuries ago by the Ancients and grinds them to temper her clay. The lucky person who gets one of Ruth's pots is actually buying a piece of today's art and pieces of the past combined into one.

A common problem with manufacturing traditional ceramics is breakage during firing. To prevent this, Ruth kneads the clay carefully and then uses a wooden spoon to flatten bubbles out of the clay.

The clay is then shaped. Traditional Pueblo potters do not use a potter's wheel; instead, they pinch the clay into shape and smooth it with gourds. A skilled potter makes this look easy, due to years of practice, but it is very difficult for a *novice* to create an even-shaped pot by hand. Ruth is so skilled in her craft that she shapes pots without even thinking of what she is doing.

After shaping, the clay must dry. This takes four days in the winter but in the summer only one day outside in sunlight. Sandpaper is then used to smooth out any rough spots.

> "A piece of pottery is just like a little baby: watch it all the time. Just tend to it a lot."
>
> —Mary Cain, Santa Clara potter, quoted in *A Guide to Pueblo Pottery*

Color finishes are next applied to the surface of the pot. The white base coat is made from sand. Black *pigment* is from crushed stone, and reddish sand makes red pigment. These powdered substances need a binder, which is gooey stuff to make the paint stick. Wild spinach juice is allowed to set for a day, thicken, and is put in an egg carton for this purpose.

Now it is time to pencil on designs. Ruth

Ruth Koyona doesn't really have to think while she forms a pot in her hands. She has been doing this so long that the clay takes shape as if by instinct.

says she just relaxes, and the designs come to her. Laguna pottery always has four sides to the overall design, signifying the four directions of the earth. Stepped designs represent clouds, and zigzags indicate lightning. Animal forms often symbolize clans. Ruth paints lizards on pots in honor of her little grandson who is Lizard Clan. The designs are carefully painted on the pot with brushes made of horsehair or yucca cactus leaves. A fine potter paints thin lines with surgeon-like skill.

Finally, the pottery must be fired. This is no simple matter. A beehive-shaped structure is made of sheep manure, and a grate placed on top of that. This is then covered with large pieces of broken pottery, and another layer of manure is placed on that. Firing takes three hours and must be done perfectly or the pots will shatter. Even if they do not break, burn marks can disfigure the design. Firing with **dung** is rather smelly, but elders say the smell purifies the village since sheep only eat clean things. Today's Pueblo potters often have to do pottery firing away from people, since most people do not share their views on sheep manure.

If they are unaware of the process involved in making Pueblo pottery, tourists may think traditional Pueblo pots are expensive. In fact, if you consider the long and difficult process of manufacturing them, Pueblo ceramics are sold for very reasonable prices indeed. When you buy traditional Native American pottery, you are buying an object with soul.

Jewelry is also an ancient Pueblo art form. More than a thousand years ago, the people we now call Hohokam made elaborate beads, rings, bracelets, and pendants. They cut and pieced together tiny pieces of turquoise, coral, and shell. Some of these raw materials were traded all the way from the Pacific Ocean. To this day, Zuni artists are known for tiny pieces of turquoise inlaid in intricate patterns on their jewelry. Today's Pueblo jewelers are also famous for their silver work.

Carlton Jamon is a cheerful man, acclaimed for his silversmith work. He has one gallery in Zuni and another in Gallup. Carlton started making jewelry when he was fourteen. His grandfather had sheep, and Carlton spent summers helping him herd, but one summer, there was no work—so he spent time with his grandmother instead. She taught him how to make

Many Pueblo potters still fire their works in an outdoor dung fire, like this one photographed by Edward Curtis eighty years ago.

Noreen Simplicio's son, Kenneth Earl Epaloose, has already established his career in art at the age of eight. He has been working with clay since he was four years old. His pottery is on display at a museum in San Diego and has appeared on the cover of a book about Pueblo potters.

jewelry, and by summer's end he was making rings. He sold the items he had made that summer and used the money to buy his first set of silver-smithing tools. He still uses the pliers he bought when he was fourteen. Carlton's own son, now thirteen, is already an award-winning silversmith.

Some of Carlton's work is done with basic hand tools, but he also uses his own high-tech processes. He's seeking a **patent** for his silver stamping process using a **jig** with shaped wire outlines. The technology has its roots in military applications.

Carlton is known for his Corn Maiden design pendants made of glittering silver, with precious stones cut and fitted for details. The design is ancient. He is also noted as the first silversmith to produce hollow silver bears, in the shape of a traditional stone fetish. The bear symbolizes power, strength, and protection.

Carlton received a special honor when he was asked to make a silver *chalice* for the Pope to use at the ceremony where Sister Katharine Drexel, who did charitable work for Pueblo Indians, was declared a saint. Carlton took two weeks to create the chalice. It incorporates Zuni designs into a traditional Christian communion cup. It is now on prominent display at the *Vatican*.

Stone animal fetishes are another traditional Pueblo art form. If properly blessed, they are believed to carry the qualities of the animal they represent. In ancient times, fetishes were objects found in nature, stones or minerals that reminded the finder of a revered animal. In the last century, fetish carvings became more artistic.

Ardale Mahooty is one of today's Pueblo Indian fetish makers. He sits by a small bench outside his home in Zuni. In front of him are pieces of rock with unusual colors and textures. Beside him, on the ground, a portable generator powers a circular grinder. As he carefully grinds the stone, figures begin to take shape—a fish, then a frog. Later, he will use a hand-held tool with special grinding and drilling attachments to smooth and detail the animals. He will drill tiny holes and insert small pieces of obsidian for eyes. Sanding and polishing complete the process. A piece of stone will become a lifelike creature.

Ardale's grandfather made fetishes with a hand grinder and sold them to neighboring Navajo shepherds. The shepherds favored bears, and they would place these by the gates of their sheep corrals for protection against predators.

In the 1960s, Indian craftsmen began putting tiny fetishes on necklaces, and these became popular with collectors of Indian art. In the 1980s, fetishes became even more popular as objects of spiritual power. Now it wasn't just Indians who wanted fetishes—the *Wall Street Journal* printed an article telling of an attorney who relied on his fetish for success in the courtroom and a stock trader who always carried his fetish bear with him to the stock exchange. When the 1980s began, there were less than twenty-four fetish carvers at work—but by 1990, more than three hundred Zuni artists were carving fetishes.

Some popular subjects that Ardale makes are frogs, lions, bears, bats, horn toads, fish, and lizards. One of the most popular Zuni fetish designs is the frog, which is associated with rain. The Corn Maiden is another traditional design. Ardale has made other designs for people who request them, such as an alligator, a scorpion, and a shark. His favorite materials are marble, pipestone, and shell.

Carlton Jamon, of Zuni Pueblo, displays an example of his silver artistry.

Carlton Jamon is especially known for his Corn Maiden pendants, made of silver with precious stone inlays.

Ardale Mahooty works outside his home in Zuni, making lifelike animal fetishes out of unusual pieces of stone.

Today, Pueblo art has become so popular that many non-Indian artists imitate its style. Imitation may be the price of success, but for Native American artists, it's a price that can ruin their livelihood. Many Native people depend on crafts—either in whole or in part—to make a living. The sales of Indian crafts each year in America may amount to about a billion dollars. Tragically, more than half those sales go to non-Indian fakers.

Counterfeit Indian art is made in Mexico, Pakistan, India, Thailand, and the Philippines. These fakes are then sold as genuine Indian art. In the past few years, the fakes have become more and more like the real article, and they have taken more and more of the profits out of Indian hands. A village in the Philippines has even been officially named Zuni, so the people there can copy Zuni Pueblo art and label these fakes "made in Zuni."

Native American artists like Carlton Jamon depend on art sales for their livelihood. When people buy fake Indian art that has been manufactured overseas, Indian artists suffer.

Edward Curtis took pictures of traditional Zuni pottery early in the twentieth century. Notice the similarities to Noreen Simplicio's work on page 68.

The pottery of modern Native artists reflects centuries of traditions.

Cheree Shebala is wearing a beautiful Zuni Squash Blossom necklace made of silver and turquoise, as part of her dance attire.

Counterfeiting Indian art is not only morally wrong; it can be devastating to Indian people's lives. Craftsmen at Santo Domingo Pueblo, famous for their intricately made *heishi* beads, have been practically put out of work by counterfeiting competitors. For some Indian artists, lost sales mean their cars have been repossessed, and in worst cases their utilities shut off in their homes.

The past is always a part of the present for the Pueblo, and the beauty of ancient structures inspires today's artists.

If you buy Indian art, make sure it is actually made by North American Indian artists. Many fakes are marketed through the mail or Internet as "Indian made." The surest way to buy the genuine article is to buy directly from the artist. Ask for a receipt stating the name of the artist and the tribe to which he or she belongs. Look for the logo of the Indian Arts and Crafts Association, an organization that carefully limits its stamp of approval to genuine Indian artists. Probably the best way to guard against purchasing counterfeit art is to acquire knowledge. If you are familiar with what you are buying, you are much less likely to be taken. And remember that age-old piece of advice—if something looks too good to be true, it probably is.

Ann Rose Ray is proud of her home—the Pueblo of Laguna. She enjoys giving tours to visitors, and meeting people at the restaurant where she works.

Chapter 7

Challenges for Today, Hopes for Tomorrow

John Ray has been a college student in Kansas, a DJ in Santa Fe . . . and now he's happy to be back with his family in Laguna. He has come back stronger, knowing what the world has to offer and, as a result, appreciating more where he comes from. He is a young man who values tradition, including the Laguna language. He looks up to the elders, who guarded his heritage through years of persecution. John has already been involved in *activism* for Indian rights, which he regards as "good training" for the rest of life. He considers himself a "positive Native American," and goes on to say: "It doesn't matter what you call us—we know who we are."

Pueblo Indians today have good reason for optimism. Over the past decades, the Pueblo have faced plenty of challenges and come out ahead. They have stepped successfully into the twenty-first century, while retaining roots in the past. They have dealt with economic, environmental, and cultural threats, and overcome them by determination and the wisdom of tradition.

Surrounded by foreign cultures, the Pueblo Indians have long struggled to achieve prosperity. The middle of the last century was an especially hard

Casinos have been called "the New Buffalo," due to their potential for providing Indians' practical needs. Not all casinos are profitable, however. The people of Laguna Pueblo see their casino and restaurant as an opportunity to let visitors know about Laguna.

time. Workers and soldiers returned home after the war to face unemployment. Ranching and crop farming, their traditional forms of employment, became unprofitable. The Pueblo met these economic challenges creatively.

One way to economic improvement has been the wise use of short-term gains, turning boom times into lasting forms of development. Before the Lagunas allowed Anaconda to mine their land, for instance, they had already attained guaranteed money for environmental restoration. Laguna Construction Company was formed to do the job of **reclamation**. Today, Laguna Construction is 100 percent Laguna owned. The company does construction management, hazardous waste removal, mine reclamation, and general construction. This reclamation industry is a solid way for the Pueblo to employ its people, and it fits well with traditional values of respect for the earth.

Another way Pueblo Indians have "seized the day" economically is by building casinos. Laguna built theirs in 1999, and today it employs two hundred tribal members. The casino restaurant gives customers a delicious taste of Laguna hospitality. Sometimes customers come in expecting to see people wearing feathers and leather outfits. They say, "Where are the Indians?" Laguna casino and restaurant workers respond to insensitive remarks with good grace. Conversations with uninformed customers are opportunities to teach others about their pueblo and their lives today. They know that casinos may not be profitable forever, and they are dedicated to wisely investing the profits into tribal *infrastructure*, social services, and educational needs. They have learned over the years to take advantage of today's opportunity by investing for the future.

Casinos have been very profitable for some tribes. Acoma and Pojoaque, for example, have seen solid improvements in the lives of their people due to casinos established in the mid-1990s. People have sturdier homes, more reliable cars, and less fear of poverty. Drinking problems have declined in Acoma, as people are freer from financial worries.

Some tribes, however, have decided against the casino business. Zuni feel that the presence of a casino would damage their traditional ways of life. The Hopi recently turned down casino development by a close vote—986 were against gambling and 714 in favor of it. Ultimately, the Hopi rejected gambling, even though backers said the casino would provide five hundred jobs and $15 million in annual profits for the tribe. The majority felt their ancient beliefs prohibited reliance on gaming. San Ildefonso, the Pueblo home of famous potter Maria Martinez, has also turned its back on gambling, choosing to rely on art sales rather than gaming for economic survival.

Pueblo Indians have always understood their destinies to be closely connected with the land. Their most earnest struggles with the outside world have been over issues of environment, especially land and water claims.

Laguna Construction Company is entirely Laguna owned. It provides jobs for Laguna people and does its work in ways that respect the earth.

Blue Lake lies in the mountains of northern New Mexico, an ancient sacred site for the Taos Pueblo community. In 1906, the U.S. government took Blue Lake and placed it under the control of the Forest Service—and the Taos Indians began a long battle for their religious freedom and protection of sacred land. A tribal representative declared: "The story of my people and the story of this place are one single story. No man can think of us without also thinking of this place. We are always joined together." It took sixty-four years of protests and legal battles, but Blue Lake was given back to Taos Pueblo in 1970. It was the first time in history that an Indian nation was given back its land for religious reasons.

The Zuni won another enormous land claim victory in 1990. In 1982, they submitted an argument to the U.S. Court of Claims, stating that between 1876 and 1939 the United States had illegally taken more than 14,000,000 acres (5,668,000 hectares) of land from the Zuni. After five years of detailed legal work, in 1987 the Court finally agreed that the government had indeed stolen vast amounts of Hopi land. For the next three years, experts worked hard to determine the value of that land. Finally, in 1990, the Zuni were awarded $25,000,000 for their stolen land. The money has been put in a trust fund for tribal development.

Recently, the Pueblo of Isleta grabbed the attention of the Environmental Protection Agency and the big city of Albuquerque when the pueblo complained about water quality in the Rio Grande River. Isleta is just south (downstream) of Albuquerque; the Rio Grande River picks up radiation

At the Hawikku Visitors' Center, an artist has drawn his idea of what Zuni might look like in the future.

Most of today's Pueblo Indians live in frame houses, often with stucco walls similar to their ancestral homes.

from the nuclear laboratories at Sandia, then industrial waste from the city, and finally flows down through Isleta Pueblo. The Isleta complained that the waters coming through their community were hazardous—and then they did something else no one expected. They presented their demands for cleaner water as a religious freedom issue. At the end of each summer, the Pueblo of Isleta gathers for a harvest ceremony. The ancient and sacred ritual involves dancing, then bathing in the Rio Grande and drinking its water. The residents of Isleta learned that low-level radioactive waste from hospitals and labs made the water unsafe even to bathe in, much less to drink. By polluting the river, these industries were preventing the Isleta Indians from practicing their traditional religion.

Perhaps the gravest threats to Pueblo people today are not economic or environmental but cultural. Exposed to the allure of twenty-first-century entertainment, some Pueblo young people are not committed to learning their language and traditions. For any group of people, keeping traditional beliefs depends on knowing the traditional language. The danger today, as one Laguna woman put it, is this: "We are so busy progressing that it's hard to take time to learn the language." Some of the larger or more isolated pueblos face little difficulty keeping their language, since it is the first language learned and spoken in homes. In other pueblos, however, people speak mostly English. Teenagers may not know their own language, or if they do, they do not speak it fluently. Certain dances and ceremonies have been discontinued, because the words for prayers have been forgotten.

Laguna, like the other pueblos, is heading into the twenty-first century with pride and courage.

Traditional languages may be making a comeback, however. **Head Start** programs are teaching very young children their traditional tongue. As tribes take greater control over their schools, **bilingual** education becomes more commonplace. There are also informal factors helping today's Pueblo Indians to maintain their traditional speech. For example, Pueblo grandparents often take care of their little grandchildren, so young parents can work and not have to pay for childcare. As the elders care for the children through the day, they speak their native language with the children. Family closeness, a virtue that has kept Pueblo people strong for centuries, is now helping them save their languages.

A century ago, anthropologists predicted the Pueblo Indians would become extinct, decimated by diseases. If they managed to avoid that sad fate, scholars said, the Indians would melt into the rest of American society—indistinguishable from people of European ancestry around them. These arrogant predictions, like so many other things falsely said about the Pueblo Indians, have proved to be false. After centuries of attack in one form or another, the Pueblo people today thrive both numerically and culturally. Their children look at the world with bright eyes. They are growing up at ease with CDs and the Internet—and equally at ease with the language, dances, crafts, and prayers of their ancestors. New generations of Pueblo Indians are about to assume their precious heritage.

Further Reading

Arnold, Caroline. *The Ancient Cliff Dwellers of Mesa Verde.* New York: Clarion, 1992.

Gibson, Daniel. *Pueblos of the Rio Grande: A Visitor's Guide.* Tucson, Ariz.: Rio Nuevo Publishers, 2001.

Lavender, David Sievert. *Mother Earth, Father Sky: Pueblo Indians of the American Southwest.* New York: Holiday House, 1998.

Noble, David Grant. *Ancient Indians of the Southwest.* Tucson, Ariz.: Southwest Parks and Monuments Association, 1998.

Noble, David Grant, and Richard B. Woodbury *Zuni and El Morro Past & Present.* Santa Fe, N.M.: Ancient City Press, 1993.

Schaafsma, Polly, ed. *Kachinas in the Pueblo World.* Salt Lake City: University of Utah Press, 2000.

Trimble, Stephen. *The People: Indians of the American Southwest.* Santa Fe, N.M.: School of American Research Press, 1993.

For More Information

Acoma Pueblo Sky City Official Site
www.puebloofacoma.org

Laguna Pueblo Official Site
www.lagunapueblo.org

Pueblo of Zuni Official Site
www.Ashiwi.org

Indian Pueblo Cultural Center
www.indianpueblo.org

Publisher's Note:

The Web sites listed on this page were active at the time of publication. The publisher is not responsible for Web sites that have changed their address or discontinued operation since the date of publication. The publisher will review and update the Web sites upon each reprint.

Glossary

activism: Taking action in support of a cause.

adobe: A building material of sun-dried earth and straw.

anthropologist: Someone who studies human beings based on their classification and the relationship of races, physical characteristics, environmental and social relations, and culture.

artifacts: Objects created by humans for practical use.

bilingual: The ability to speak and understand two languages.

chalice: A ceremonial goblet, often used for communion.

conquistadors: Spanish conquerors.

consensus: A general agreement within a group.

constitutions: The basic principles and laws of a nation, state, or social organization.

criteria: Standards on which decisions or judgments are made.

democratic: A form of government based on rule by the common people and focusing on social equality.

desecrate: To treat disrespectfully; to violate the sanctity of something.

diphtheria: A contagious disease that produces a toxin causing inflammation of the heart and nervous system.

diverse: Having different characteristics.

domination: Supremacy over another.

dung: Manure.

emergence: The act of coming into view.

epidemics: Diseases affecting a large number of people at the same time.

fetishes: An object, usually a carving of an animal, believed to have magical powers for its owner and having the characteristics of the subject of the carving.

harmony: A pleasing arrangement of parts.

Head Start: A government program providing pre-kindergarten education programs for children whose families meet income guidelines.

immunity: The condition of being able to resist a particular disease.

infrastructure: The system of public works of a country, state, or region (roads, water lines, and septic systems, for example).

ingenuity: Skill or cleverness in combining things; inventiveness.

jig: A device used to maintain the correct position between a piece of work and a tool, or between pieces of work during assembly.

liaison: A close bond or relationship.

lynched: Hanged.

majordomos: Persons who speak, make arrangements, or take charge for another.

matriarch: A female who rules or dominates a family or group.

medicine man: A spiritual leader.

mediums: Materials, such as stone or paint, used for artistic expression.

mesas: Isolated high ground that is relatively flat-topped.

mica: Any of various colored or transparent mineral silicates that easily separate into layers.

New Agers: People who participate in the social movement of the late twentieth century and early twenty-first century that drew from ancient concepts, especially Eastern and Native American traditions.

novice: A beginner.

obsidian: A dark natural glass formed by cooling molten lava.

optimism: The tendency to look at the best of everything and for the best possible outcome.

patent: A legal document providing the inventor the exclusive right to make, use, or sell an invention for a specified number of years.

pigment: The substance that provides color.

pillaging: The act of looting, especially during war.

plaza: A public square.

practicality: Usefulness.

reclamation: The act of restoring to its previous condition.

savvy: Understanding; practical know-how.

smallpox: A contagious disease characterized by skin eruptions and scarring.

stucco: A material made of cement, sand, and a small amount of lime which is applied to the outside walls of buildings.

taboo: Something that is forbidden because of supernatural, spiritual, or moral reasons.

traditional: Having to do with the way one's ancestors did things.

uranium: A heavy radioactive element.

Vatican: The Pope's headquarters in Rome.

venerate: To honor with a ritual act of devotion.

Index

Biographies

Kenneth McIntosh is a pastor. He took a leave from his regular job to work on this series. Formerly, he worked as a junior high school teacher in Los Angeles, California. He wrote *Clergy* for the Mason Crest series "Careers with Character." He lives in upstate New York with his wife and two children, Jonathan and Eirené. He is grateful for the opportunity this work has given him to travel and meet with many wonderful Native people.

Martha McCollough received her bachelor's and master's degrees in anthropology at the University of Alaska-Fairbanks, and she now teaches at the University of Nebraska. Her areas of study are contemporary Native American issues, ethnohistory, and the political and economic issues that surround encounters between North American Indians and Euroamericans.

Benjamin Stewart, a graduate of Alfred University, is a freelance photographer and graphic artist. He traveled across North America to take the photographs included in this series.